THE

Eugene Ionesco was born in
French. His work includes *Th*
Bald Prima Donna.

Martin Crimp was born in 1956. His plays include *Definitely the Bahamas* (1987), *Dealing with Clair* (1988), *Play with Repeats* (1989), *No One Sees the Video* (1990), *Getting Attention* (1991), *The Treatment* (winner of the 1993 John Whiting Award) and *Attempts on her Life* (1997). A short fiction, *Stage Kiss,* was published in 1991. His work for radio includes the Giles Cooper Award-winning *Three Attempted Acts* (1985) and the original version of *Definitely the Bahamas,* winner of the 1986 Radio Times Drama Award.

EUGENE IONESCO

The Chairs

translated by Martin Crimp

faber and faber

First published in this translation in 1997
by Faber and Faber Limited
3 Queen Square London WC1N 3AU

Photoset by Faber and Faber
Printed in England by
CPI Antony Rowe, Chippenham, Wiltshire

Martin Crimp is hereby identified as translator of this
work in accordance with Section 77 of the Copyright,
Designs and Patents Act 1988

A CIP record for this book
is available from the British Library

ISBN 978 0571 19451 3

6 8 10 9 7 5

Characters

Old Man, 95 years old
Old Woman, 94 years old
Orator, 45–50 years old
Plus many other characters

Set: Circular walls with a recess at the back.

A very bare room. Stage right, starting from down-stage, are three doors. Then a window with a step-ladder in front of it. Then one more door. In the recess up-stage is a large, palatial double door, with two more doors facing each other on either side of it. These two doors, or one of them at least, are almost hidden from the audience. Stage left – again beginning from down-stage – are three doors, a window with a step-ladder opposite the one on the other side, then a blackboard and a rostrum. The plan overleaf will make this clearer.

Down-stage, two chairs side by side.

A gas-lamp hangs from the ceiling.

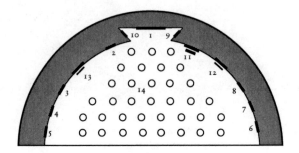

1 Large double door
2, 3, 4, 5 Side doors (stage right)
6, 7, 8 Side doors (stage left)
9, 10 Doors hidden in recess
11 Rostrum and blackboard
12, 13 Windows (with step-ladders in front)
14 Empty chairs

The shaded area represents a corridor (off stage)

The curtain rises. Semi-darkness. The Old Man, standing on the ladder, leans out of the window, stage right. The Old Woman is lighting the gas-lamp. Green light. She goes and tugs at the Old Man's sleeve.

Old Woman Please – poppet – shut the window. You're letting the stench of stagnant water in. Not to mention the mosquitoes.

Old Man Don't bother me now.

Old Woman Please – please – poppet – come and sit down. Stop leaning out. You might fall in. Remember what happened to Henry the Seventh. You can never be too careful.

Old Man Spare me your historical examples, petty-pie. I'm sick to death of Tudor history. I like looking out. The little boats are like sunspots.

Old Woman There aren't any little boats. There isn't any sun. It's night-time, popsy.

Old Man There's still the afterglow. (*He leans right out.*)

Old Woman (*grabbing on to him*) No poppet! You're frightening me. Come and sit down. You'll never see them coming when it's dark out.

The Old Man reluctantly allows himself to be dragged away.

Old Man But I wanted to watch. I so love watching water.

Old Woman But how *can* you, you poor poppet? Just thinking of it makes my head spin. This house – my God – this island – I'll never get used to it. To be surrounded by water . . . from under the window-ledges right up to the horizon.

The Old Woman drags the Old Man towards the two chairs down-stage. The latter sits quite naturally on the former's lap.

Old Man Six in the evening – and already dark. It didn't used to be like this. Not in the old days. Remember? It could be light at nine, or ten, or even midnight.

Old Woman You're absolutely right – what a memory!

Old Man Things have changed.

Old Woman And why would you say that was?

Old Man I've no notion, petty-pie. Perhaps because the further we go, the deeper we sink. What with the way the world goes round and round and round and round . . .

Old Woman And round and round, my poppet. (*Silence.*) Yes – my God – you have such a penetrating intelligence. Such gifts, poppet! You might've been a master of the arts, master of the rolls or have masterminded a military campaign – if you'd had the will, if you'd just had some inkling of ambition.

Old Man And what use would that've been? It wouldn't've improved life. Besides, I'm master enough. A janitor. Master of the mop and bucket.

Old Woman (*stroking him like a child*) My poor poor darling popsy.

Old Man I'm very fed up.

Old Woman You were happier watching the water.
    Why don't you 'be' something to cheer us up?

Old Man Why don't *you* 'be' something – it's your turn.

Old Woman Oh no it's not.

Old Man Oh yes it is.

Old Woman Isn't.

Old Man Is.

Old Woman Isn't.

Old Man Finish your tea, Sémiramis.

There is no tea – obviously.

Old Woman How about doing February.

Old Man I hate February.

Old Woman Well, then do me another one. Please. Pretty pretty please.

Old Man All right. Look: February. (*He scratches his head like Stan Laurel.*)

Old Woman (*laughing and clapping*) Perfect! Thank you, thank you, my perfect darling poppet! (*Kisses him.*) Such gifts! Yes, you might've been so masterful, if you'd only tried . . .

Old Man Master of the mop, you mean. And bucket.

Silence.

Old Woman Tell me a story. Go on. Do 'the two of us came'.

Old Man What? Again? I'm sick of 'the two of us came'. It's all you ever ask for! 'The two of us came'. It's just too tedious. Seventy-five years of married life and every evening without exception you're still forcing me to tell the same old story, impersonate the same old characters, do the same old months . . . on and on and on. Can't we change the subject?

Old Woman But Popsy, I don't find it tedious. It's your life. It fascinates me.

3

Old Man You know it from memory.

Old Woman But the moment it's over, it all feels forgotten. Every evening I come to it afresh. Honestly, poppet. It's a technique. I purge myself. I refresh myself. Every night, my poppet. Just for you.
  Do it. Please.

Old Man If you insist.

Old Woman I do insist. Tell me your story. Because your story is my story too. 'The two of us came . . .'

Old Man 'The two of us came. . .', petty-pie.

Old Woman 'The two of us came. . .', poppety-poppet.

Old Man The two of us came to a great metal gate. We'd been soaked and frozen to the marrow for hours – days – nights – weeks on end . . .

Old Woman For months on end.

Old Man . . . by the rain. Our teeth, gums, lips, tongues, were all chattering . . . and had been for eighty years. They wouldn't let us in. They might at least have opened the garden gate.

Silence.

Old Woman In the garden the grass was wet.

Old Man A footpath led to a little square. At its centre: a village church.
  Where was that village? D'you remember?

Old Woman No, pops. Not any more.

Old Man How did we get there? What was the road? It was a place, I believe, called Paris.

Old Woman There was never any such place as Paris, pops.

4

Old Man There was such a place, only it turned to ruins. It was the city of light, only the light died, and had been dead for four hundred thousand years. There's nothing left of it now but a song.

Old Woman A song? Really? How odd. What song?

Old Man A lullaby. An allegory. 'Paris will always be Paris'.

Old Woman And you had to go through the garden? Was it far?

Old Man (*lost in a dream*) The song? . . . Or the rain?

Old Woman Such great gifts. If you'd only had some inkling of ambition, you might've been a schoolmaster, or a band master, or a concert master of medicine. But all that disappeared into the depths . . . the black depths of despair. Into the black – yes – depths.

Silence.

Old Man The two of us came . . .

Old Woman Yes! Go on. That's it.

As the Old Man speaks the Old Woman begins to laugh. At first with soft senility, but then with increasing abandon, the Old Man also laughing.

Old Man The two of us came over sick with laughter – it was such a strange story – the stranger coming thicker and faster – bare-chested, bare-fisted, he suddenly came with his bag full of tricks, sowing the seeds of laughter, thicker and stranger, stranger and faster – we suddenly came, came, came, strangely barefaced, sowing the seeds of disaster, thicker, faster, stranger, laughter at the story of disaster – sick, thick, sick with laughter the barefaced stranger suddenly came . . .

5

Old Woman (*laughing*) Suddenly overcome with laughter the stark-naked stranger's bag, the bag, the bag of tricks, thicker and stranger and faster . . .

The Old Woman and Old Man speak together:

Old Woman . . . the laughter. Yes! Came. Yes! Thicker . . . Faster . . . Naked . . . Master . . . Became . . . Disaster . . . Yes! (*growing calmer*) Came . . . yes . . . came . . . yes . . . at last . . . suddenly . . . came . . .

Old Man Suddenly, suddenly, suddenly . . . Barefaced. Yes! Bare-fisted. Yes! Sowing the seeds . . . (*growing calmer*) of disaster . . . came at last . . . yes . . . to the last . . . yes . . . to the last . . . to the last . . . laugh.

Old Woman So much then for your so-called Paris.

Old Man I couldn't agree more.

Old Woman But poppet, you're just so incredibly – what? – so incredibly, incredibly . . . I mean you could've *achieved* something in life, have mastered far more than the mere mop and bucket.

Old Man Can't we just be happy with the little we have?

Old Woman But what if you've missed your true calling?

Old Man (*bursts into tears*) Missed it? Wrecked my life? I want my mummy. Mummy. Where's my mummy? I'm an orphan. (*Moans.*) Fatherless . . . motherless . . .

Old Woman You've got me. Why be afraid?

Old Man No, petty-pie. You're not my mummy. Motherless, fatherless, who's going to shelter me?

Old Woman But I'm right beside you, poppet.

Old Man It's not the same. I want mummy. You're not my mummy.

Old Woman (*strokes him*) Darling, you're breaking my heart. Don't cry.

Old Man Don't touch me. I'm in too much pain. It's my calling. I missed it and it hurts.

Old Woman There, there . . .

Old Man (*sobbing, mouth wide open like a baby*) Motherless, fatherless . . .

Old Woman (*cuddles and tries to calm him*) You poor, darling, orphaned poppet, my heart bleeds for you. (*She rocks the Old Man, who is now sitting on her lap.*)

Old Man (*sobs*) Mummy. Where's my mummy? No more mummy.

Old Woman I'm your wife. I'm your mummy now.

Old Man (*giving in a little*) Not true, I'm a little lost orphan.

Old Woman (*still rocking him*) You poor, poor, father-less, motherless, sisterless, brotherless darling.

Old Man (*still sulking, but gradually giving in*) Won't. Won't. Don't want to. Won't.

Old Woman (*like a lullaby*) Little lost orphan, last little orphan, diddle diddle darling . . .

Old Man Won't . . . won't . . .

Old Woman Little, little darling, lonely little darling, hey diddle diddle sleep fast little orphan, last little orphan, little lost orphan . . .

Old Man (*snivels and gradually calms down*) Where *is* my mummy then?

Old Woman In a heaven decked with flowers. She can hear you. She can see you. You're not to cry – or she will!

Old Man Don't believe you . . . she can't see me . . . she can't hear me. I'm all alone. You're not my mummy.

Old Woman (*the Old Man is nearly pacified*) There there. Calm down. Don't get so upset. You're a very special person, little soldier. Wipe your eyes. Your guests are due tonight. They mustn't see you like this. Not everything's wrecked and spoiled. When you see them, you must explain. That you have a message. You've always said that you have a message. And that's why you have to live. And why you have to fight.

Old Man You're right. I must fight. I have a message. A mission. Something deep inside. A message to share with the whole of humanity.

Old Woman The whole, my poppet, of humanity!

Old Man Exactly. Yes. Exactly.

Old Woman (*wipes his nose and dries his eyes*) Exactly. As a man. As a soldier. As master among men.

Old Man (*gets off her lap and takes small, restless paces*) I'm not like other people. I have ideals. You're right: maybe I do have gifts and talent – just not the skill to apply them. I've done my duty as janitor honourably. No situation has ever defeated me. Perhaps that's enough.

Old Woman Not for you. You really aren't like other people. You're in a different class. Although, that said, life might've been more tolerable if you'd been less intolerant. You've fallen out with all your friends, masters of this, masters of that, even with your own brother.

Old Man That wasn't my fault, Sémiramis. You know quite well what he said.

8

Old Woman Which was?

Old Man Which was: 'I've caught a virus, so I came to see you in the hope it might prove infectious.'

Old Woman That's just the way people talk, sweetheart. You shouldn't've taken it so seriously. But what about Carel? Why did you lose your temper with him? Was that his fault too?

Old Man I'm going to get very very angry with you. See if I don't. Of course it was his fault. He turns up one evening and says, 'Good luck, old boy. Or like we say in the business: Break an effing leg – 'scuse my French.' Then laughs his fat head off.

Old Woman But he meant well, poppet. It doesn't do to be so sensitive.

Old Man I don't like that kind of language.

Old Woman You might've been a master craftsman or a master of disguise. Chess grand master of the hunt.

Long silence. They remain stiff and motionless on their chairs.

Old Man (*as if in a dream*) There at the end of the end of the garden lay . . . lay . . . lay . . . lay what, sweetest heart?

Old Woman Lay Paris!

Old Man At the end. At the end of the end of Paris there lay . . .

Old Woman Lay what, poor poppet? Lay who, poor poppet?

Old Man It was a time and a place of perfection.

Old Woman So perfect? Was it?

9

Old Man I can't recall where exactly . . .

Old Woman Rest your poor mind now . . .

Old Man It's too far away, too far away . . . to grasp. Where could it be?

Old Woman Could what be?

Old Man The thing . . . the thing that I . . . Where could it be? Or who?

Old Woman Wherever it is, I'll come with you, poppet. Wherever or whoever.

Old Man Oh God, it's so hard to put things into words . . . Yet everything must be spoken.

Old Woman It's a sacred duty. You have no right not to reveal your message. Mankind is waiting. The universe hangs on your lips.

Old Man All right, all right, I'll do it.

Old Woman Really and truly? I do hope so.

Old Man Finish your tea.

Old Woman You might've been a master of oratory if you'd just been stronger willed. I'm so proud and happy that you've finally made the decision to address nations – Europe – whole continents!

Old Man If only I could put things into inevitable-sounding words.

Old Woman Once you've started it'll sound inevitable enough – like living and dying. The decision is everything. Speaking itself brings words and ideas into existence – and maybe you and I, through our words, can rediscover the city, and the garden, and not be orphans any more.

Old Man I won't be doing the talking. I've hired a professional Orator to speak on my behalf – as you will see.

Old Woman You mean it's really happening tonight? Well I hope you've invited everyone – all the big names – all the property developers and experts.

Old Man Oh yes – all the property developers and experts.

Silence.

Old Woman What – chemists? Violinists? Trouble-makers? Boiler-makers? Scaffolding erectors? Associate directors? Politicians? Televisions? Spin doctors? Helicopters?

Old Man Yes yes yes – miners, artists and designers – everyone with a little expertise and an interest in property!

Old Woman Bankers?

Old Man Well, obviously.

Old Woman Post-Marxists, neo-Nazis, fundamentalists, environmentalists? Therapists and therapees?

Old Man Well yes yes yes, of course – since they all amount to property developers and experts.

Old Woman Calm down, popsy. I didn't mean to upset you. It's just you tend to be careless – like all great geniuses. Tonight's meeting is important. They all need to be there. Can you count on them? Did they promise?

Old Man Finish your tea, Sémiramis.

Silence.

Old Woman Pope Paul and the popular press?

Old Man Well obviously. (*Silence.*) Well obviously I'm going to pass my message on to them. My whole life has been spent suffocating. But now, thanks to you and the

Orator – the only ones to understand me – all will be revealed.

Old Woman I'm so proud of you.

Old Man The meeting will begin in a few minutes.

Old Woman You mean they really are coming *tonight*? Then you won't need to cry any more: instead of mummies and daddies you'll have property developers and experts. (*Silence*.) You don't think the meeting should be adjourned? You don't think it will be too tiring?

> *More pronounced agitation. Already the Old Man has begun to pace round the Old Woman, taking small uncertain steps, like the very young or the very old. Perhaps he takes one or two steps towards one of the doors, then comes back and paces round.*

Old Man You really think it might be tiring?

Old Woman You do have a slight cold.

Old Man But how could we cancel?

Old Woman Invite them another night. Telephone.

Old Man Good God, it's far too late for that. They'll already have started out.

Old Woman You should've thought of that.

> *The sound of a boat cutting through the water.*

Old Man I think someone's already here . . . (*The sound grows louder*.) Yes! Listen!

> *The Old Woman also gets up and limps about.*

Old Woman Perhaps it's the Orator.

Old Man He wouldn't come so soon. It must be someone else.

A bell rings.

Ah!

Old Woman Ah!

Nervously, they head for the hidden door, up-stage left, talking as they go.

Old Man Come on, come on . . .

Old Woman I look like a haystack . . . Wait a moment . . . (*Limping along, she sorts out her hair and her dress, and pulls up her thick red stockings.*)

Old Man You should've thought of that earlier. You had plenty of time.

Old Woman Just look at this old dress . . . it's creased to pieces . . .

Old Man Then you should've ironed it. Hurry up! You're keeping them waiting.

Followed by the grumbling Old Woman, the Old Man reaches the hidden door and they both, briefly, disappear. We hear them open the door, then shut it after letting someone in.

Voice of Old Man Hello. Good evening. Please come inside. We're delighted to meet you. This is my wife . . .

Voice of Old Woman Hello. Good evening. So pleased you could come. Mind you don't crumple your hat. Take out the pin and put it down. But of course no one will sit on it.

Voice of Old Man Allow me to help you off with your mink. What? Oh, it'll be quite safe here with us.

Voice of Old Woman What a beautiful suit! Such a brave use of colour! Can I interest you in a cracker? . . . But

13

you're not overweight, it's just . . . puppy fat.

I'll take your umbrella.

Voice of Old Man If you'd like to come this way . . . (*He reappears, back to the audience.*) It's all rather spartan, I'm afraid.

The Old Man and the Old Woman turn round together and move a little apart to make room for the guest. She is invisible.
The Old Man and the Old Woman then come downstage, in conversation with the invisible Lady.

Old Man (*to invisible Lady*) And how was the weather?

Old Woman (*as above*) Tiring journey? . . . You must be exhausted.

Old Man (*as above*) What? On the beach?

Old Woman (*as above*) You really are too kind.

Old Man (*as above*) Let me get you a chair. (*He moves stage right and exits through door no. 6.*)

Old Woman (*as above*) Take this one for now. (*She indicates one of the two chairs and sits in the other, on the invisible Lady's right.*) Hot, isn't it? (*She smiles at the Lady.*) What a lovely fan! My husband . . .

The Old Man reappears in door no. 7 with a chair.

. . . gave me something similar seventy-three years ago . . . I've still got it . . .

The Old Man puts the chair on the invisible Lady's left.

It was a birthday present.

The Old Man sits on the chair he's just brought in, meaning the invisible Lady is in the middle. The Old Man, turning to the Lady, smiles and nods, rubs his hands, and seems to follow what she says. Old Woman likewise.

Old Man Living, dear lady, has never been cheap.

Old Woman (*to Lady*) You're so right . . .

The Lady speaks.

Absolutely. The world will have to change . . . (*Changes tone.*) I think my husband will be leading the way . . . he's the one to ask.

Old Man (*to Old Woman*) Not now, not now, Sémiramis. It's not the right moment. (*to Lady*) Forgive me, dear lady, if your curiosity has been aroused.

The Lady reacts.

No, I'm afraid that's something I'm not at liberty to reveal . . .

The two old people smile – laugh even. They seem to be very happily listening to a story told by the invisible Lady. Then a pause. A hiatus in the conversation. Their faces become devoid of expression.

Old Man (*to Lady*) Of course you're absolutely right.

Old Woman Absolutely, yes . . . well no, absolutely not.

Old Man Well absolutely – yes – not.

Old Woman Are you sure?

Old Man Surely not!

Old Woman Well you said it.

Old Man (*laughs*) Unbelievable!

Old Woman (*laughs*) How extraordinary! (*to Old Man*) She's a delight.

Old Man (*to Old Woman*) I see you've been charmed. (*to Lady*) Congratulations!

Old Woman (*to Lady*) You're not at all like most young women today.

The Old Man pathetically bends down to pick up an invisible object dropped by the invisible Lady.

Old Man Please . . . Don't get up . . . I can reach . . . Ah – you were too quick. (*He straightens up.*)

Old Woman (*to Old Man*) Well, she's not geriatric.

Old Man (*to Lady*) Old age is a bitter cross. May you remain forever young.

Old Woman (*to same*) And he means that from the bottom of his heart. (*to Old Man*) My darling poppet!

A few moments of silence. The old people, in profile to the audience, watch the Lady, smiling politely. Then they face the audience. Then turn again to the Lady, smiling in reply to her smile – then answering her questions with the following:

It's very kind of you to take an interest.

Old Man We live very quietly.

Old Woman He doesn't dislike people, but he does value his privacy.

Old Man We have the radio – I fish – and of course there's a pretty good boat service.

Old Woman Two on Sunday mornings, and one on Sunday evenings – and that's not counting private sailings.

Old Man (*to Lady*) On clear days we have the moon.

Old Woman (*to same*) He's still a full-time master of the mop. Which keeps him out of trouble. Although at his age

16

– you're right – he could afford to put his feet up.

Old Man (*to Lady*) Plenty of time for that when I'm dead and buried.

Old Woman (*to Old Man*) Don't say that, poppet . . . (*to Lady*) Our family – what's left of it – and my husband's friends still used to pay the occasional visit – ten years ago . . .

Old Man (*to Lady*) Wintertime – a good book – snuggled up to the radiator – with a whole life's memories . . .

Old Woman (*to Lady*) A humble life, but a full one . . . He works on his message two hours a day.

Doorbell. For a short while another boat has been heard cutting through the water.

(*to Old Man*) Hurry up. The door.

Old Man (*to Lady*) You must excuse me. It's the door. (*to Old Woman*) Quickly – fetch some more chairs.

Old Woman (*to Lady*) I won't be a moment, my dear.

Violent ringing at the door.
The Old Man, bent double, hurries to the door, stage left, while the Old Woman heads as fast as she can, limping, towards the hidden door, stage right.

Old Man Clearly someone in authority.

The Old Man hurries to open door no. 2. The invisible Field Marshal enters. Maybe it would help to discreetly hear a few notes on a trumpet – such as the tune 'Salut au Colonel'.
As soon as he opens the door and sees the invisible Field Marshal, the Old Man freezes respectfully at attention.

Ah! The Field Marshal! (*He raises his hand in the vague*

direction of his forehead, in a salute that doesn't quite happen.) Good evening, Field Marshal. This is the most incredible honour . . . it's . . . it's . . . completely unexpected . . . although . . . naturally . . . well, let's just say it is a privilege to welcome into my modest abode a hero of your stature. (*He shakes the invisible Field Marshal by the invisible proffered hand and bows with ceremony.*) Although I think I might without false modesty be permitted to declare myself not unworthy of your visit. Proud – yes. Unworthy – no.

The Old Woman appears, stage left, with a chair.

Old Woman Oh, what a heavenly uniform! What beautiful decorations! Who is he, poppet?

Old Man (*to Old Woman*) What – don't you recognize the Field Marshal?

Old Woman (*to Old Man*) Of course!

Old Man (*to Old Woman*) Count the stripes! (*to Field Marshal*) This is my wife – Sémiramis. (*to Old Woman*) Come here and I'll introduce you to the Field Marshal. (*The Old Woman comes over, dragging the chair behind her, and curtseys without letting go of it. To Field Marshal*) My wife. (*to Old Woman*) The Field Marshal.

Old Woman Quite ravished, Field Marshal. Do make yourself at home. Of course, my husband's also distinguished himself in many campaigns . . .

Old Man (*irritated*) . . . mostly against cockroaches.

The invisible Field Marshal kisses the Old Woman's hand. We realize this from the way she appears to raise her hand up to his lips. Overcome, she drops the chair.

Old Woman Such impeccable manners! Obviously a man of enormous, enormous distinction! (*She picks up the* *chair. To Field Marshal*) This chair is yours . . .

Old Man (*to invisible Field Marshal*) Please come this way . . .

They all move down-stage, the Old Woman dragging the chair.

That's right – someone's already arrived. No doubt the first of many!

The Old Woman sets the chair stage left.

Old Woman (*to Field Marshal*) Please. Do sit down.

The Old Man introduces the two invisible characters to each other.

Old Man A young lady friend of ours . . .

Old Woman A very close young lady friend of ours . . .

Old Man And this distinguished gentleman . . . is the Field Marshal.

Old Woman (*indicating to the Field Marshal the chair she's brought*) Why don't you sit down?

Old Man (*to Old Woman*) But can't you see the Field Marshal wants to sit next to the young lady . . .?

The Field Marshal sits invisibly in the third chair from the left – the invisible young Lady sitting supposedly in the second. An inaudible conversation begins between the two invisible characters. The two old people remain standing behind their chairs, on either side of the two invisible guests. Old Man, stage-right, beside the Lady, Old Woman, stage-left, beside the Field Marshal.

Old Woman (*listening to the guests' conversation*) Really! He's going too far.

Old Man (*also listening*) Quite possibly.

The Old Man and the Old Woman make signs to each other over their guests' heads while at the same time listening to their conversation with increasing concern. Suddenly:

No, Field Marshal. They're not here yet. They're on their way. An orator is going to speak on my behalf and explain my message . . . Please, Field Marshal. This young lady's husband could arrive at any moment.

Old Woman (*to Old Man*) Who *is* this person?

Old Man (*to Old Woman*) I told you: it's the Field Marshal.

Socially unacceptable acts are invisibly occurring.

Old Woman (*to Old Man*) I knew that.

Old Man So why did you ask?

Old Woman To find out of course. Field Marshal – not on the floor please! Use the ashtray.

Old Man (*to Field Marshal*) Field Marshal, refresh my memory. The last war – did you win it or lose it?

Old Woman (*to invisible Lady*) You silly girl – don't be talked into it!

Old Man Just look me in the eyes – do I look like a coward? One day, Field Marshal, in the thick of battle . . .

Old Woman It's not decent! There are limits! (*She tugs at the Field Marshal's invisible sleeve.*) Listen to him! Poppet! Make him stop!

Old Man (*quickly going on*) . . . in the thick of battle I killed two hundred of the buggers single-handed . . . Thick they were, like flies. Not a pretty sight. But thanks to my strength of character, Field Marshal, I had the bastards . . .

Please! No! Stop! Enough is enough!

Old Woman (*to Field Marshal*) My husband never lies. We may be old, but at least we're respectable.

Old Man (*to Field Marshal, violently*) The perfect hero should also have perfect manners!

Old Woman (*to Field Marshal*) In all the long years I've known you, I would never have believed you could stoop so low. (*to the Lady, as more boats are heard*) I would never have believed he could stoop so low. There is such a thing as dignity – and self-respect.

Old Man (*very quavering voice*) I'm still quite capable of handling a weapon, you know. (*doorbell*) Excuse me. The door. (*He makes an awkward move and knocks over the invisible Lady's chair.*) I'm so sorry!

Old Woman (*rushing over*) Have you hurt yourself?

They help the invisible Lady to her feet.

You're all covered in dust. (*She helps the Lady brush off the dust. Doorbell again.*)

Old Man I'm so terribly, terribly sorry. (*to Old Woman*) Fetch another chair.

Old Woman (*to the invisible pair*) Excuse us one moment.

While the Old Man goes to open door no. 3, the Old Woman exits for a chair via door no. 5 and reappears via door no. 8.

Old Man (*heading for the door*) He was trying to infuriate me. And he nearly succeeded. (*Opens the door.*) My God, what are *you* doing here? I can hardly believe my eyes – but yes, how utterly unexpected – it really is – the very same selfsame woman. I've spent a life – a *lifetime* –

thinking about you – the belle, the belle, we called you, of the ball – the fabulous Beauty . . . And this must be the Beast, I mean your husband. Of course. Yes. Married. But you haven't changed at all . . . Or rather, my God, yes! Your unfortunate nose! It's grown like a hose-pipe. I didn't notice at first but now the terrible length of it is staring me in the face. But what a shame! Still, these things can't be helped . . . So how did it happen? . . . I see: gradually. My dear friend – if I may call you that – you must forgive me only I knew your wife long before you did . . . Oh yes – she was just the same – apart from the hose, I mean nose . . . My congratulations. You both seem very much in love.

The Old Woman appears at door no. 8 with a chair.

Sémiramis – there are two of them – we need another chair.

The Old Woman puts down the chair behind the existing row, then exits through door no. 8 returning after a few moments through door no. 5 with another one. She puts this beside the first, by which time the Old Man and the two new guests will have come down to her.

Please. Come inside. We already have a little gathering. I'll introduce you. Well well well, it's 'the belle' as we used to call you, '*Mademoiselle*' . . . Bent double now . . . But yes, of course, still beautiful as ever. Eyes still twinkling over the cataracts. Hair still cascading over the patches of pink scalp. Come along, come along . . . And what's this? A present for my wife? (*to the Old Woman who has just arrived with the chair*) Sémiramis. This is her. Remember? Our fabled Beauty . . . (*to Field Marshal and first invisible Lady*) May I introduce you both to a legendary beauty – please don't snigger – and her husband. (*to Old Woman*) This is the childhood friend I've often mentioned – and her husband. (*once more to Field*

Marshal and first invisible Lady) And her husband . . .

Old Woman *(curtseys)* Well . . . clearly a man of some distinction. Good evening, Beauty. Good evening, husband. *(pointing out the other invisible guests to the newcomers)* That's right – friends of ours.

Old Man *(to Old Woman)* He's brought you a present.

The Old Woman takes the present.

Old Woman Let me guess. Is it a . . . man? Or a tree? Is it a lamb? Or a bumble-bee?

Old Man *(to Old Woman)* Rubbish. It's a picture.

Old Woman Of course! A picture. How lovely! Thank you so much. *(to first invisible Lady)* My dear, you can look at it if you want.

Old Man *(to invisible Field Marshal)* You can look at it too if you want.

Old Woman *(to husband of Fabled Beauty)* Doctor, doctor, my pulse races, my face is all hot, I need an operation, I've no sensation in my feet, frozen fingers, frozen eyes, doctor, doctor, what do you advise . . .?

Old Man *(to Old Woman)* This gentleman isn't a doctor, he's an offsetlithographer.

Old Woman *(to first Lady)* If you've finished looking, you can hang it up. *(to Old Man)* Well, offset or not, he's still charming – if not dazzlingly handsome. *(to Offsetlithographer)* You weren't supposed to hear that.

The old couple should now be behind the chairs, almost touching, but back to back. The Old Man speaks to the Fabled Beauty, the Old Woman to the Offsetlithographer. They occasionally turn to deliver a line to one of the first guests.

23

Old Man I am profoundly moved . . . You're still the same woman, in spite of all . . . A hundred years ago I used to love you . . . You've changed so much . . . Yet haven't changed at all . . . I loved you then, and love you now . . .

Old Woman (*to Offsetlithographer*) No no no. You weren't. You really weren't. You really, really weren't.

Old Man (*to Field Marshal*) I quite agree with you there.

Old Woman (*to Offsetlithographer*) No no no. You really weren't supposed to hear. (*to first Lady*) Thank you for putting it up . . . I'm sorry if it was inconvenient.

The light is now stronger. It grows and grows as the other guests arrive.

Old Man (*almost sobbing, to Fabled Beauty*) Where are the snows of yesteryear?

Old Woman (*to Offsetlithographer*) You really weren't. You absolutely, really, really weren't.

Old Man (*pointing to first lady*) A young lady friend of ours . . . she's rather quiet . . .

Old Woman (*pointing to the Field Marshal*) Yes, the Field Marshal's a kind of mounted elder statesman . . . my husband's friend, but naturally not his equal . . .

Old Man (*to Fabled Beauty*) But your ears weren't always pointed! . . . Poor beauty, don't you remember?

The Old Woman behaves increasingly grotesquely towards the Offsetlithographer as the scene progresses. She simperingly shows her thick red stockings, lifts her numerous skirts, reveals her moth-eaten petticoat, exposes her old woman's breasts. Then, hands on hips, head flung back, shrieking erotically, she thrusts her pelvis out, legs apart, and laughs the laugh of an old whore. This behaviour – quite different from anything we've seen or have yet to see, and which should reveal a hidden aspect of the Old Woman's personality – will abruptly end.

Old Woman Surely at my age it's not physically possible? What? You disagree?

Old Man (*to Fabled Beauty, very romantic*) In our day the moon was a live star. My God – yes! – if we had only dared – but we were such children. Shall we try and make up the time we've lost? Could we? Would we? No, never in a thousand years. Time has raced past like a train, engraving its lines across our skin. Might cosmetic surgery be the answer? (*to Field Marshal*) We're both of us soldiers, and soldiers are forever young – the military are like gods . . . (*to Fabled Beauty*) It shouldn't've been like this . . . my God, my God, everything thrown away. We might've known such happiness, such incredible, incredible happiness. Might snowdrops yet bloom beneath the snow? . . .

Old Woman (*to Offsetlithographer*) You naughty naughty flatterer. Look younger than I am? You wicked boy. You're making me hot.

Old Man (*to Fabled Beauty*) Shall I be Tristan to your Isolde? Beauty resides in the soul . . . Don't you realize? Joy, beauty, eternity itself might all have been ours . . . If we had only dared. We were too weak-willed. We threw it all, all, all away.

Old Woman (*to Offsetlithographer*) Don't don't don't don't don't. You're making me shudder all over. Are you shuddering too? Or is that a sensitive shiver? This is embarrassing . . . (*She laughs.*) D'you like my petticoat? Or are you a stocking man?

Old Man (*to Fabled Beauty*) A wretched life spent wielding a mop and bucket.

Old Woman (*turns to first invisible Lady*) For pie in the sky? Take a vat of fat, a sheet of meat and the juice of a goose. (*to Offsetlithographer*) Oh yes – just let your fingers linger . . . Oh yes – like that . . . ah . . .

Old Man (*to Fabled Beauty*) Sémiramis, with all due modesty, has taken my mother's place. (*Turns to Field Marshal.*) But Colonel, surely I must've said: Truth is truth, no matter where you find it.

Old Woman (*to Offsetlithographer*) You honestly think a woman can have children *of* any age *at* any age?

Old Man (*to Fabled Beauty*) An inner world, an inner calm, abstinence, scientific and philosophical investigation, my message – these are what have kept me sane . . .

Old Woman (*to Offsetlithographer*) I've still never been unfaithful . . . not so hard, you'll have me on the floor . . . I'm just his unfortunate mother! (*Sobs.*) A distant, distant, (*pushing him away*) distant . . . relation. These cries . . . are the cries of conscience. Life's roses aren't for me to gather. Find some other path to happiness. Time's wingèd chariot has passed us by.

Old Man (*to Fabled Beauty*) . . . a life devoted to superior concerns . . .

The Old Man and the Old Woman lead Fabled Beauty and Offsetlithographer to the other invisible guests and get them to sit.

Old Man and Old Woman Please, please, sit down.

The old couple sit, he on the left, she on the right, with the four empty chairs between them. A long silent scene, occasionally punctuated by 'yes', 'no', 'yes', 'no'.[1] *The old people are listening to what the invisible characters are saying.*

26

Old Woman (*to Offsetlithographer*) We had a son . . . very much alive, yes . . . he left us . . . a common enough story . . . well, actually quite strange . . . he deserted his parents . . . such a good-natured boy . . . a long time ago now . . . To love someone so much . . . and have them slam the door in your face . . . My husband and I tried to force him to stay . . . he was seven – the age of reason – we were screaming at him: Come back, son, come back, son, come back . . . He didn't even turn his head.

Old Man I'm afraid not . . . I'm afraid we never had children . . . I would've liked a son . . . so would Sémiramis . . . we tried everything . . . and Sémiramis, poor thing, is so maternal . . . Perhaps it was for the best. Having been a terrible son myself . . . Pain, regrets, remorse, that's all there is, that's all that's left.

Old Woman He said: You're killing the birds! Why are you killing the birds? . . . We're not killing the birds . . . we'd never hurt a fly . . . Great tears in his eyes. Which he wouldn't let us wipe. You couldn't go near him. He said: Yes you are, yes you are killing the birds, killing them all . . . Brandishing his tiny fists at us . . . Liars! You tricked me! The streets are full of murdered birds, little dying children. But the birds are singing! . . . No, those are cries of agony. The sky's red with blood . . . You silly boy – the sky is blue . . . But he kept screaming: You tricked me, I loved you, I thought you were good . . . the streets are full of dead birds, you've poked their eyes out . . . Naughty Mummy! Naughty Daddy! . . . I can't live here any more . . . I went down on my knees . . . His father was sobbing. We couldn't stop him . . . *Then* he shouts: I hold you responsible . . . Responsible? What does *that* mean?

Old Man I left mother to die alone in a ditch. I could hear her pathetic groans: My little child, my beloved son, don't leave me all alone to die . . . Stay with me. I don't have much time left. Don't you worry, Mother, I said, I'll be back in no time . . . I was in a hurry . . . I had a party to go to. 'I'll be back in no time.' When I returned she was already dead and deeply buried . . . I dug up the earth to look for her . . . but I never found her . . . Of course, of course, sons always desert their mothers and end up killing their fathers . . . Such is life . . . But I feel the pain . . . when others don't . . .

Old Woman He was calling: Mummy – Daddy – I'll never see you again . . .

Old Man I feel the pain, you see, when others don't.

Old Woman Please don't mention this to my husband. A man who so dearly loved his parents. Who never left their sides. Who cared for and cherished them . . . They died in his arms, saying: You've been the perfect son. May God reward you.

Old Man I can still see her lying in the ditch, with lilies in her hand, crying out: Don't forget me, don't forget me . . . There were great tears in her eyes, and she called me her poppet. Little poppet, she said, don't leave me all alone, not here.

Old Woman (*to Offsetlithographer*) He's never written. Once in a while a friend says he's seen him somewhere or other, that he's doing well, that he's a good husband and so on and so forth . . .

Old Man (*to Fabled Beauty*) When I returned she was already long buried. (*to first lady*) But of course we do! The house has its own cinema, restaurant and several en suite bathrooms . . .

Old Woman (*to Field Marshal*) Exactly, Field Marshal. The reason is: he . . .

Old Man Basically that's the reason.

28

Disconnected conversation grinding to a halt.

Old Woman Let's hope so!

Old Man Which is why I . . . why he . . . Obviously.

Old Woman (*fragmented dialogue: exhaustion*) In other words.

Old Man For us and for our family.

Old Woman Such that one.

Old Man I gave it him.

Old Woman Gave whom what?

Old Man Them.

Old Woman In a paper bag . . . can you believe it.

Old Man It's not a matter of.

Old Woman Why?

Old Man Yes.

Old Woman I.

Old Man In other words.

Old Woman In other words.

Old Man (*to first lady*) I'm sorry: did you speak?

*For a few moments the old people remain frozen in
their chairs. Then the bell goes again.*

(*with mounting agitation*) They're coming. Guests. More
guests.

Old Woman I thought I heard boats . . .

Old Man I'll go. You get the chairs. Ladies and gentlemen, if you'll excuse me. (*He heads for door no. 7.*)

Old Woman (*to invisible characters already present*) Can I ask you all to get up for a moment. The Orator is due very soon. We need to get the room ready for the lecture. (*She arranges the chairs with their backs to the auditorium.*) If you wouldn't mind helping me . . . Thank you.

Old Man (*opening door no. 7*) Evening, ladies. Evening, everyone. Please do come in.

> *The three or four invisible new arrivals are very tall and the Old Man has to stand on tiptoe to shake their hands.*
> *The Old Woman, after arranging the chairs as described above, comes behind the Old Man.*

(*making introductions*) Evening. Thank you. This is my wife. Evening. Thank you. This is my wife. Evening. Thank you. This is my wife.

Old Woman Who are all these people, poppet?

Old Man (*to Old Woman*) Fetch some chairs, sweetheart.

Old Woman I can't do everything! . . .

> *She exits, grumbling, through door no. 6, and returns through door no. 7. Meanwhile the Old Man brings the new arrivals down-stage.*

Old Man Don't drop your film equipment . . . (*more introductions*) The Field Marshal . . . A young lady-friend . . . Our Fabled Beauty . . . Our Offsetlithographer . . . These are journalists who've also come to hear our speaker – who will undoubtedly be here at any moment . . . Please don't be impatient . . . You won't get bored – you have each other . . .

> *The Old Woman appears with two chairs at door no. 7.*

Come on now, hurry up with those chairs . . . We need another one.

Still grumbling, the Old Woman goes to fetch another chair, exiting through door no. 3 and returning through no. 8.

Old Woman All right, all right . . . I'm doing the best I can . . . I'm not a piece of machinery . . . Who are all these people? (*She exits.*)

Old Man Please: take your seats – ladies with the ladies, gentlemen with the gentlemen – or the opposite if you prefer . . . No, we don't have any nicer chairs . . . it's all a bit improvised . . . excuse me . . . have this one in the middle . . . What? You need a pen? . . . For an outside line? Just dial 9 . . . I don't have a television . . . but I do get all the papers . . . well that depends on lots of things: I run the building, but I don't have the staff . . . we're forced to economize . . . I'm sorry: no interviews – not yet . . . later – possibly . . . you need a seat immediately? . . . well where's she got to? . . .

The Old Woman appears in door no. 8 with a chair.

Hurry up, Sémiramis . . .

Old Woman I'm doing my best . . . Who are all these people?

Old Man I'll explain later.

Old Woman And that woman? Who's that woman, Poppet?

Old Man Nothing to worry about . . . (*to Field Marshal*) The journalist's profession, Field Marshal, is very like the soldier's . . . (*to Old Woman*) Take care of the ladies, sweetheart, will you . . . (*Doorbell. He hurries for door no. 8*) Wait one moment . . . (*to Old Woman*) Chairs!

Old Woman Excuse me, ladies and gentlemen . . .

The Old Woman exits through door no. 3 and returns

through no. 2. The Old Man goes to open concealed door no. 9 and vanishes just as she reappears through no. 2.

Old Man (*unseen*) Come in . . . come in . . . come in . . . come in . . . (*He reappears, followed by a number of invisible people including a tiny child whose hand he holds.*) You don't bring young children to scientific lectures . . . he'll get bored, poor thing . . . all we need is for him to start screaming or piddling over the ladies' dresses!

The Old Man leads them centre-stage. The Old Woman arrives with the chairs.

This is my wife. Sémiramis: these are their children.

Old Woman Evening, ladies. Evening, everyone. Oh – aren't they charming!

Old Man This is the youngest.

Old Woman Oh, how utterly utterly sweet!

Old Man Not enough chairs.

Old Woman Oh dear oh dear oh dear oh dear . . . (*She goes out for another chair. She now uses doors 2 and 3 on the right for entrances and exits.*)

Old Man Put the toddler on your lap. The twins can share a chair. Careful – they're a bit wobbly . . . they came with the house, they belong to the owner. That's right, children – he's a nasty little man – he'd like us to buy them off him – but we're not forking out for his old junk.

The Old Woman arrives as fast as she can with a chair.

You don't all know each other . . . this is the first time you've met . . . you used to all know each other's names . . . (*to Old Woman*) Sémiramis, help me make the introductions . . .

Old Woman Who are all these people? . . . May I present – excuse me – may I present . . . but present who?

Old Man Allow me to present . . . May I present . . . This is Mr and Mrs – Would you like to meet – good. Wonderful. Can I introduce you to –

Old Woman (*to Old Man*) Did you put a vest on? (*to invisible guests*) Very pleased. Very very pleased. Very very pleased to meet you.

Doorbell rings.

Old Man Guests!

Doorbell rings.

Old Woman More guests!

Doorbell rings again. Then again and again. The Old Man is overwhelmed. The chairs, now facing the rostrum, backs to the auditorium, create regular and ever-growing rows like theatre seats. The Old Man, out of breath, mops his brow and goes between the doors, arranging the invisible people, while the Old Woman hobbles as best and as fast as she can from one door to another, fetching and carrying chairs. There are now many invisible guests on stage. The old ones are careful not to bump into people as they thread their way along the rows of chairs. The sequence might be this:
The Old Man goes to door no. 4, Old Woman exits through no. 3, returns through no. 2. The Old Man goes to open no. 7, Old Woman exits through no. 8, returns through no. 6 with chairs, etc. – in order to move round the whole stage, using all the doors.

Excuse me . . . excuse me . . . what? . . . yes . . . sorry . . . sorry . . .

Old Man Evening, ladies. Evening, gentlemen. Evening,

33

everyone. What? Yes. Sorry. Evening. Evening . . .

Old Woman (*with chairs*) There . . . there . . . there are just . . . there are just too many of them . . . no no no no no . . .

From outside the increasingly loud and increasingly close sound of boats cutting through the water. All these sounds now come only from the wings. The Old Woman and the Old Man continue the actions indicated above – opening doors, bringing chairs. The ringing is continuous.

Old Man This table's in our way.[2] (*Without slowing down, he moves, or rather appears to move a table, helped by the Old Woman.*) There's hardly any room to move – excuse us . . .

Old Woman (*appearing to get rid of the table. To Old Man*) Did you put a vest on?

Bell goes repeatedly.

Old Man More guests! More chairs! More guests! More chairs! Evening ladies. Evening everyone. Sémiramis, hurry up . . . Someone will surely help you . . .

Old Woman Excuse me . . . excuse me . . . Very pleased. Yes yes yes yes. Very very pleased. Yes yes yes, the chairs . . .

The Old Man – while the bell gets louder and louder and we hear boats knocking more and more often against the nearby quayside – gets tangled up in the chairs and hardly has time to get from one door to the next, so rapidly does each ring follow the other.

Old Man Yes I'm coming . . . did you put a vest on? Yes yes, coming coming . . . yes yes . . . coming coming . . .

Old Woman Vest on? What vest on? . . . excuse me, excuse me . . .

Old Man This way, everybody . . . You must . . . you must – sorry – excuse me . . . come in, come in . . . just follow . . . seats over here . . . my dear girl . . . not over there . . . take care . . . call yourself a friend? . . .

Then, for a long while, no more words. We hear the waves, the boats, the endless ringing. The action is at its highest intensity. All the doors now open and close continuously of their own accord. The great double door at the back remains closed. The old couple go from one door to another, silently. They seem to be gliding on skates. The Old Man welcomes the guests and shows them in, but without going very far – only taking one or two steps with them and pointing out their seats – there's no time to do more. The Old Woman brings on chairs. The Old Man and the Old Woman meet and collide once or twice without interrupting the action. Then, up-stage centre, the Old Man, almost without moving, turns from left to right, from right to left, etc., pointing out seats. Rapid pointing. Then, finally, the Old Woman stops, chair in hand, puts down the chair, picks it up again, puts it down again, and appears to act as if she wished to go from one door to another, right to left, left to right, rapidly moving her head and neck. The movement mustn't slacken: the old couple must give the impression of never stopping, even though almost rooted to the spot. Their hands, their torsos, their heads, their eyes move restlessly, perhaps describing circles. Eventually the action begins to slow down, imperceptibly but progressively. The ringing is less frequent and less loud. The doors open less and less rapidly. The old couple's gestures progressively slow down. By the time the doors have completely stopped opening and shutting, and the bell stopped ringing, we should feel that the stage is totally jam-packed with people.[3]

I'll find you a seat . . . patience now . . . Sémiramis, what in God's name . . .

Old Woman (*big empty-handed gesture*) There are no more chairs, my poppet. (*Then suddenly she starts to sell invisible programmes in the packed room/auditorium with its closed doors.*) Programmes, get your programmes here, programmes for tonight, get your programmes here!

Old Man Patience, ladies and gentlemen, please. Someone will deal with you . . . Everyone will be dealt with in order of arrival . . . Places will be found. Arrangements made.

Old Woman Get your programmes here! One moment please, young lady, I can't serve everyone at once, I'm not made of arms, I'm not an octopus . . . If the man over there would be good enough to pass this one to the lady next to him – thank you . . . and the change please . . .

Old Man If I promise you a seat you'll get a seat! Just keep your hair on! This way, that's right, careful . . . yes, dear friend . . . my dear, dear friends . . .

Old Woman . . . programmes . . . getcha programmes . . . getcha, getcha . . .

Old Man Of course she's here – further back – selling programmes . . . every job counts, however humble . . . that's her . . . see her? . . . there's a seat for you in the second row . . . on the right . . . I mean left . . . got it!

Old Woman getcha grammes . . . getcha programmes . . . getcha programmes here . . .

Old Man Well, what d'you want me to do about it? I'm doing my best! (*to the invisibly seated*) Can you all bunch up a bit . . . one tiny gap, Madam, if you can squeeze into it, come on. (*To avoid the crowd he's obliged to climb on to the rostrum.*) Ladies and gentlemen, our apologies – but it's now standing room only . . .

Old Woman (*who is at the other end, opposite the Old Man, between door no. 3 and the window*) Getcha programmes . . . anyone for programmes? Choc-ice, toffees . . . extra-strong mints . . . (*Trapped by the crowd, unable to move, she throws programmes and sweets at random over invisible heads.*) Catch! Catch! Catch! Catch!

The Old Man stands excitedly on the rostrum. He is jostled and gets down – climbs back up, climbs back down – hits someone in the face, gets elbowed, speaks:

Old Man Excuse me . . . I'm so sorry . . . be careful . . . (*In the crush, he staggers and has difficulty keeping his balance – he grabs on to people's shoulders.*)

Old Woman Who on earth are all these people? Programmes, getcha programmes, ice-creams. Catch! Catch! Catch! Catch!

Old Man Ladies and gentlemen, can I please ask you for a moment's silence . . . I said silence . . . this is very important . . . would those people without seats please keep the gangways clear . . . thank you . . . Please don't stand between the chairs.

Old Woman (*almost screaming*) Who are all these people, poppet? What are they doing here?

Old Man Please clear the gangways. In everyone's best interest, would people without seats please stand over here, or over there, against the walls . . . Don't worry, you'll be able to see and hear everything – there are no bad seats!

Great commotion: propelled by the crowd, the Old Man almost does a circuit of the stage until ending up by the window, stage left, near the step-ladder. The Old Woman completes a similar circuit in the opposite

37

direction, ending up by the window, stage right, near the other step-ladder.

Old Man (*as he moves*) No need to push, no need to push, no need to push.

Old Woman (*as she moves*) No need to push, no need to push, no need to push.

Old Man (*as he moves*) No need to push, no need to push, no need to push.

Old Woman (*as she moves*) No need to push, ladies and gentlemen, no need to push.

Old Man (*as he moves*) A little sanity . . . a little care . . . a little sanity . . .

Old Woman (*as she moves*) You could at least behave like civilized people.

At last they reach their definitive positions, each beside a window, the Old Man, stage left, beside the window on the rostrum side, the Old Woman, stage right. They remain in these positions till the end.

(*calling her husband*) Poppet . . . I can't see you any more . . . where are you? Who are they all? What do they all want? Who's that over there?

Old Man Where are you? Where are you, Sémiramis?

Old Woman Poppet, where are you?

Old Man Over here, by the window . . . can you hear me? . . .

Old Woman Yes! I can hear your voice! . . . I can make it out . . . Among the many . . .

Old Man And where are you?

Old Woman I'm by the window too! . . . I'm frightened,

38

sweetest heart, it's too crowded . . . we're so far apart . . .
at our age we should be more careful . . . we should keep
together . . . we might lose each other . . . you just never
know, my poor poor poppet . . .

Old Man Ah! . . . There you are . . . oh, we'll meet again,
never fear . . . I'm with friends! (*to friends*) I'm delighted
to shake hands with you . . . Well, of course I believe in
the inevitability of progress – though not without the
occasional hiccup . . .

Old Woman Very well, thank you . . . Such terrible
weather! Such a beautiful day! (*to herself*) But I'm still
afraid . . . What am I doing here? (*Shouts.*) Poppet!
Popsy!

Each speaks to the guests on their side.

Old Man To end man's inhumanity to man we need
limitless limitless limitless cash.

Old Woman Poppet! (*then cornered by friends*) Of course
my husband's here – he's the organizer . . . over there . . .
No, you'd never make it . . . you'd have to get to the
other side, where his friends are . . .

Old Man Certainly not . . . I've always held that logical
positivism is positively illogical.

Old Woman You do get these so-called happy people.
Breakfast on the plane, lunch on the train, dinner on an
ocean liner. They sleep on trucks that roll on and on and
on through the night . . .

Old Man Human dignity? Let's save face first and talk
about dignity afterwards.

Old Woman Don't slip in the dark. (*She bursts out laughing mid-conversation.*)

Old Man It's what the public want.

Old Woman Absolutely. Spare me no detail.

Old Man I've invited you here . . . to tell you the whole story . . . the personal individual is one and the same thing as the individual person.

Old Woman If he looks sheepish, it's because he owes us money.

Old Man I am not I. I am another. I am the one contained within the other.

Old Woman Each child must learn to hate the other.

Old Man Sometimes I wake up surrounded by silence. At the centre of a crystal sphere. But beware. At any moment the bubble can burst into a thousand fragments.

Old Woman Fragments, phantoms, figments . . . My husband's role is very important, if not sublime.

Old Man I'm sorry . . . I completely disagree! . . . You'll be informed in due time of my thinking on the subject . . . For now my lips are sealed! . . . The man we're waiting for – the Orator – he's the one who'll deal with all these burning issues . . . He'll explain everything . . . When? . . . When the moment comes . . . as the moment soon will . . .

Old Woman (*to her friends*) And the sooner the better . . . (*to herself*) Why can't they go away and leave us alone? . . . Where's my poor poppet – he's vanished . . .

Old Man (*to his friends*) There's no need for that attitude. You'll hear my message presently.

Old Woman (*to herself*) Ah! That's his voice! . . . (*to her friends*) My husband, you know, has always been misunderstood. At last his hour has come.

Old Man Listen. I have acquired enormous experience. In all areas of life, and of philosophy . . . Not for personal gain, but for the benefit of humanity.

Old Woman Ouch! You're treading on my corns.

Old Man I have perfected an entire system. (*to himself*) The Orator should be here! (*aloud*) I have suffered greatly.

Old Woman We have suffered much. (*to herself*) The Orator should be here! Surely it's time.

Old Man Suffered much. Learned much.

Old Woman (*like an echo*) Suffered much. Learned much.

Old Man You'll see for yourselves: my system is perfect.

Old Woman (*like an echo*) You'll see for yourselves: his system is perfect.

Old Man Provided you obey my instructions.

Old Woman (*echo*) Provided you follow the instructions.

Old Man We can save the world! . . .

Old Woman (*echo*) Save his soul and save the world! . . .

Old Man One truth for all.

Old Woman (*echo*) One truth for all!

Old Man You will obey me! . . .

Old Woman (*echo*) You will obey him! . . .

Old Man Since my authority is absolute! . . .

Old Woman (*echo*) His authority is absolute! . . .

Old Man Never . . .

Old Woman (*echo*) Never, never, never . . .

Suddenly from the wings, noise and fanfares.

What's happening?

The sounds get louder, then the door at the back opens wide with an enormous din. Through the open door we see only a void, but from it an intense light floods the stage. With the arrival of the equally invisible Emperor, the windows are also brightly lit.

Old Man Incredible . . . unimaginable . . . is it possible? . . . my God . . . my God . . . unbelievable . . . and yet so – no – so – no – yes! The Emperor! His Majesty the King of Kings!

Light at maximum intensity through the windows and the open door – but cold, empty light. More noise which abruptly ends.

Old Woman Poppet . . . oh poppet . . . who is it?

Old Man Please stand! . . . The Emperor! The King of Kings! In my house. In our house . . . Sémiramis . . . can't you see?

Old Woman (*not understanding*) King of what Kings, my poppet? (*Then suddenly understands.*) But of course – the Emperor! The King! The King of Kings! (*She curtseys frantically, endlessly.*) In our very own house!

Old Man (*weeping with emotion*) Majesty! . . . Oh my Majesty! . . . Oh my darling, oh my divine Majesty! . . . Such grace sublime! . . . Such an incredible dream . . .

Old Woman (*echo*) Incredible dream . . . inedible dream . . .

Old Man (*to invisible crowd*) Ladies and gentlemen, will you all please stand. Our beloved sovereign the King of Kings is in our midst! Hip hip. Hooray! Hip hip. Hooray! Hip hip. Hooray!

He climbs the step-ladder and stands on tiptoe to

*glimpse the Emperor. On the other side the Old
Woman does the same.*

Old Woman Hip hip. Hooray! Hip hip. Hooray! Hip hip.
Hooray!

Stamping of feet.

Old Man Your Majesty! . . . I am here! . . . Can Your
Majesty hear me? Can you see me? Please inform His
Majesty that I am here! Majesty! Majesty! I am here –
your most faithful servant! . . .

Old Woman (*still as echo*) Your most faithful servant,
Majesty!

Old Man Servant. Slave. Dog. (*He howls.*) Your dog,
Your Majesty . . .

The Old Woman also howls loudly like a dog.

(*wringing his hands*) Can you see me? Answer, my Lord!
. . . Yes! A glimpse! I've just glimpsed Your Majesty's
noble face . . . your divine brow . . . Glimpsed it, yes,
despite the screen of sycophants . . .

Old Woman Despite the sycophants . . . we are here, oh
Lord.

Old Man Majesty! Majesty! Please – all of you – don't
leave His Majesty just standing there . . . You see, Lord,
I'm the only one who cares for you, for your well-being,
most faithful of your subjects . . .

Old Woman (*echo*) Your Majesty's two most faithful subjects!

Old Man So let me through, ladies and gentlemen . . .
How can I clear a way through this crowd? . . . I have to
offer His Majesty the Emperor my most humble respects
. . . Let me through . . .

Old Woman (*echo*) Let him through . . . let him through . . . do . . . do . . . do . . .

Old Man Let me through, do, do, do let me through. (*desperately*) Oh, will I never reach him?

Old Woman (*echo*) Reach him . . . reach him . . .

Old Man I lay my heart and my whole being at his feet. But the sycophants surround him. Oh yes – they want to stop me reaching him . . . They all have suspicious minds . . . Don't think I'm blind . . . I know an intrigue when I see one . . . They want to keep Your Majesty and me apart!

Old Woman Not so loud, poppet . . . His Majesty's watching you . . . His Majesty winked at me . . . The Lord is on our side! . . .

Old Man Give our Lord the best seat . . . near the rostrum . . . so he can hear the Orator's every word.

The Old Woman, on tiptoes on her ladder, strains her head back as far as she can to see.

Old Woman At last they're taking care of the Emperor.

Old Man Heaven be praised. (*to Emperor*) My Lord . . . you may rest assured, that man beside you is a friend and deputy. (*on tiptoe, standing on ladder*) Ladies and gentlemen, *Mesdames et Messieurs*, girls and boys . . . I beg you . . .

Old Woman (*echo*) Beg you . . . egg you . . .

Old Man . . . to let me see . . . to move apart . . . to let me see . . . his celestial gaze . . . his worthy face, his crown, his halo of majesty . . . Lord, deign to turn your illustrious eyes upon your humble, humble servant . . . Yes! This time I can see him really clearly . . .

Old Woman (*echo*) This time really . . . really . . . really clearly . . .

Old Man What pinnacle of bliss! . . . What words could express my overwhelming gratitude! . . . to have here – yes, here in my modest abode – His Majesty! Yes! Light of my life! – in this abode where I too am master of a kind, a kind of king, king of the mop . . .

Old Woman (*echo*) . . . and bucket, bucket, bucket . . .

Old Man And proud to be . . . proud and at the same time humble . . . as is fitting . . . Yes! I too might've belonged to the master-class, might've ruled not scrubbed the corridors of power . . . Your Majesty, words . . . words don't come easily . . . I might've had . . . many things . . . wealth . . . if I'd only sought, if I'd only thought, if only I . . . if only we . . . Lord, forgive my confusion . . .

Old Woman More formal!

Old Man (*snivelling*) I mean: may our Lord deign to grant forgiveness! You really came . . . we'd abandoned hope . . . we might not have been here . . . Oh! Saviour! My life has been humiliating . . .

Old Woman (*echo, sobbing*) . . . miliating . . . waiting . . . waiting . . .

Old Man A life full of suffering . . . I might have been a somebody, if I'd been sure of Your Majesty's support . . . I have no support . . . if you hadn't come, it would all have been too late . . . You, Lord, are my life's last hope . . .

Old Woman (*echo*) . . . life's last . . . Lord's last . . . hope's last . . .

Old Man I've brought misfortune on my friends, on all those who helped me . . . Lightning would strike the out-stretched helping hand . . .

Old Woman (*echo*) . . . hands outstretched . . . fetched . . . retched . . .

Old Man I was always hated for the right reasons and loved for the wrong ones . . .

Old Woman Not true, poppet. *I* love you – I'm your little mother . . .

Old Man All my enemies made the grade while my friends betrayed me . . .

Old Woman (*echo*) Betrayed . . . the grade . . . the grade . . . betrayed . . .

Old Man They hurt me. They persecuted me. If I protested, right was always on their side. Sometimes I tried to take revenge . . . but I could never, never avenge myself . . . I felt too much pity . . . I could never tread the enemy underfoot, I was always far too nice.

Old Woman (*echo*) Far far far far far too nice . . .

Old Man Pity got the better of me . . .

Old Woman (*echo*) Pity me . . . pity me . . . pity me . . .

Old Man But they had no pity. If I so much as pricked them with a pin they clubbed me, knifed me, shot me, pulverized my bones . . .

Old Woman (*echo*) . . . pulverize . . . eyes . . . eyes . . . eyes . . .

Old Man They usurped me, robbed me, murdered me . . . I was a collector of disasters, a conductor of catastrophes . . .

Old Woman (*echo*) lightning . . . lightning . . . lightning conductor . . .

Old Man In order to forget, Your Majesty, I took up

sport . . . rock-climbing . . . but they grabbed my ankles and made me slip . . . I tried to climb the stairs instead, but they collapsed in a heap of rotting wood . . . I tried to travel, but they refused me a passport . . . I tried to cross the river, but they burnt my bridges . . .

Old Woman (*echo*) Burnt his bridges.

Old Man I tried to cross the Pyrenees, but the Pyrenees were no more.

Old Woman (*echo*) No more Pyrenees . . . He too, Your Majesty, might've been a master of ceremonies, master chief petty officer of the navy, or have even painted a major masterpiece . . .

Old Man What's more, no one ever considered my feelings . . . or invited me to dinner . . . While I – and I hope you're listening to me – while I alone might have saved humanity from terminal decline – which Your Majesty must also recognize . . . Or I might at least have spared it the evils it has endured this last quarter of a century, given the chance to communicate my message. Not that I despair of saving it still. There is still time and my plan is to . . . I'm sorry, I'm not putting this very clearly . . .

Old Woman (*over invisible heads*) The Orator will be here, he'll do the talking. His Majesty is here . . . so people will listen, you mustn't worry any more, you hold the winning hand, things have changed, they've changed . . .

Old Man Please forgive me . . . Your Majesty has more important concerns . . . I've been humiliated . . . Ladies and gentlemen, please make a tiny space, don't entirely obliterate from sight His Majesty's nose, I want to see the diamonds glinting on the celestial crown . . . But if His Majesty deigns to enter my wretched home, it surely means he condescends to have some regard for my poor self. Extraordinary recompense indeed. And if, Your

47

Majesty, my body stands on tiptoe, this is not through pride, but only the better to behold you! . . . Since my soul grovels at your feet . . .

Old Woman (*sobbing*) Yes, Lord. We grovel at your feet, at your heels, at your toes . . .

Old Man I was afflicted by boils. The foreman sacked me because I wouldn't simper over his baby or slobber over his horse. They kicked me up the arse, my Lord. But none of that matters now . . . because . . . My Lord . . . this way . . . I'm over here . . .

Old Woman (*echo*) Over here . . . over here . . . over here . . .

Old Man Because Your Majesty is here . . . Because Your Majesty will give my message due consideration . . . But the Orator should be here . . . He's keeping Your Majesty waiting . . .

Old Woman His Majesty must forgive him. He is due. He'll be here any moment. There was a phone-call.

Old Man The Lord is bountiful. The Lord won't just up and leave without even listening.

Old Woman (*echo*) . . . even . . . even . . . even listening . . .

Old Man He's the one who'll speak for me . . . I'm not capable . . . I'm not talented . . . he's got all the documents, all the files . . .

Old Woman Just be patient, Lord, we beg of you . . . He is due . . . He's due at any moment.

Old Man (*so the Emperor doesn't get bored*) Listen, Your Majesty – a long time ago I had a revelation . . . I was forty years old . . . in fact this story will interest everyone . . . Well, one evening, after eating and before going to bed, I was sitting as I usually did on my father's lap . . .

My moustache was bigger than his and had pointier ends
. . . I had a hairier chest . . . my hair was already going
grey, whereas his was still brown . . . We had guests –
important people – eating with us – and they all started
laughing like maniacs . . .

Old Woman (*echo*) Axe . . . axe . . . axe . . .

Old Man It's not a joke, I told them. I like my daddy
very much. They said to me: But it's gone midnight. Little
boys don't go to bed this late. If one is not yet in beddy-
byes, then one cannot be a kiddy-wink, can one. I
wouldn't've taken them seriously if they hadn't been so
formal . . .

Old Woman (*echo*) Formal . . .

Old Man Not like normal . . .

Old Woman (*echo*) Normal . . .

Old Man All the same, I thought, I'm not married. So I
must be a child. So they married me off that very instant,
just to prove me wrong. Fortunately my wife has taken
the place of a mother and father . . . [4]

Old Woman The Orator is due, Your Majesty . . .

Old Man The Orator is coming.

Old Woman Is coming.

Old Man Is coming.

Old Woman Is coming.

Old Man Is coming.

Old Woman Is coming.

Old Man Is coming, is coming.

Old Woman Is coming, is coming.

Old Man Is coming.

Old Woman He comes.

Old Man He comes.

Old Woman He comes. He's here.

Old Man He comes. He's here.

Old Woman He comes. He's here.

Old Man and Old Woman He's here . . .

Old Woman He's here!

Silence. All movement stops.

Transfixed, the old couple stare at door no. 5. This motionless scene lasts for some time – about half a minute. Then, very very slowly, the door opens wide in complete silence – and the Orator appears – a 'real' character. He resembles a nineteenth-century painter or poet: broad-brimmed felt hat, cravat, jacket, moustache and goatee – self-important – a poseur. If the invisible characters should seem as real as possible, the Orator, conversely, appears unreal. Clinging to the wall, stage right, he moves slowly to the back, in front of the great door, seeming to glide, without turning his head to either side. He passes close to the Old Woman, but appears not to notice her, even when she touches his sleeve to confirm that he exists and says:

He's here!

Old Man He's here!

Old Woman (*unable to take her eyes off him*) He's really here. He's really real. As large as life.

Old Man (*staring*) He's really real. And really here. It's not a dream!

Old Woman I told you it wasn't a dream.

The Old Man clasps his hands and raises his eyes to heaven in silent exultation. The Orator, when he arrives up-stage, removes his hat, bows in silence – a cross between a musketeer and an automaton – and doffs his hat to the invisible Emperor.

Old Man Your Majesty . . . may I present the Orator . . .

Old Woman He's really here!

Then the Orator puts his hat back on and mounts the rostrum where, from on high, he surveys the invisible audience and the chairs. He freezes in a solemn pose.

Old Man (*to invisible audience*) You may ask for his autograph.

Automatically and in silence the Orator signs and distributes innumerable autographs. Meanwhile the Old Man raises his eyes again to heaven, joins his hands, and says with exultation.

No man in his lifetime could hope for more . . .

Old Woman (*echo*) No man could hope for more.

Old Man (*to invisible crowd*) And now with Your Majesty's permission I turn to all of you – ladies and gentlemen, boys and girls, tiny tiny children, colleagues, countrymen, Mr Chairman, comrades-in-arms . . .

Old Woman (*echo*) Tiny . . . tiny . . . tiny . . . tiny . . . children.

Old Man I turn to all of you, regardless of age, sex, class, race or sexual orientation, to thank you from the bottom of my heart.

Old Woman (*echo*) Thank you . . . thank you . . .

Old Man And the Orator too . . . most warmly . . . for this enormous turn-out . . . Silence, gentlemen, please! . . .

Old Woman (*echo*) Gentlemen, please . . . gentlemen, please . . .

Old Man I also wish to thank all those who have made this evening's gathering possible. The organizers . . .

Old Woman Hear! Hear!

The Orator meanwhile remains solemn and motionless on the rostrum. Only his hand continues automatically signing autographs.

Old Man The owners of this building. The architect. The builders who were kind enough to raise these walls! . . .

Old Woman (*echo*) . . . raze these walls . . .

Old Man And all those who dug the foundations . . . Silence, ladies and gentlemen, please!

Old Woman (*echo*) . . . ladies and gentlemen, please . . .

Old Man Not forgetting our sincerest thanks to the joiners who made the very chairs you're sitting on, the craftsman by whose skill . . .

Old Woman (*echo*) . . . kill . . . kill . . .

Old Man . . . was constructed the armchair in which His Majesty so softly flops – without in any way compromising his mental rigour – and thanks to the technicians, electricians and stage mismanagers . . .

Old Woman (*echo*) . . . mismanagers, anagers . . .

Old Man . . . to the paper manufacturers, printers, proof-readers and sub-sub-editors to whom we owe the prettily designed programmes. Our thanks to the worldwide solidarity of man, to our country, to the ship of state (*turning to the Emperor*) which His Majesty pilots like a true professional . . . Thanks to the most luscious of ushers . . .

Old Woman (*echo*) . . . the ushers are luscious . . .

Old Man (*pointing to the Old Woman*) Who sells the programmes and sweetly blushes . . .

Old Woman (*echo*) . . . luscious, ushers, blushes . . .

Old Man . . . my wife, my life . . . Sémiramis! . . .

Old Woman (*echo*) . . . my wife . . . my life . . . (*to herself*) My poppet never forgets me.

Old Man Thanks to all those who have offered their precious and professional moral or financial support, thus contributing to the total success of this evening's event . . . And thanks again, thanks above all to our beloved Sovereign, the King of Kings . . .

Old Woman (*echo*) . . . of Kings, of Kings . . .

Old Man (*in complete silence*) . . . A moment's silence . . . Oh Lord . . .

Old Woman . . . oh Lord, oh Lord . . .

Old Man Oh Lord and Majesty, my wife and I ask nothing more of life. Our existence may now end in this blaze of glory . . . We thank the heavens for granting us so many long, quiet years . . . My life has been a full one. My mission is accomplished. I shall not have lived in vain now that my message can be revealed to the world.

The Old Man gestures towards the Orator who is oblivious – repelling requests for autographs with forceful dignity.

To the world – or rather to what's left of it! (*broad gesture to invisible crowd*) To you in other words, dear friends, the left-overs of humanity – but with left-overs such as these we can still work miracles in the kitchen . . . My dear Orator . . .

The Orator is looking elsewhere.

If I have for so long been disregarded, disenfranchised, by my contemporaries, then such was my fate.

The Old Woman sobs.

What does any of that now matter when to you, my dear friend and Orator . . .

The Orator rejects another autograph request – then looks all around, striking a pose of indifference.

. . . falls the task of lighting posterity's path by the lamp of my intelligence? . . . Acquaint therefore the Universe with my philosophy. Leave out no detail of my private life – albeit harrowing, touching, or bizarre – my curious appetites . . . my perverse desires . . . reveal them all . . . Speak of my companion . . .

The Old Woman's sobs redouble.

. . . of her unsurpassable smothered liver hot-pots, of her unique stuffed bellies of pickled pork . . . Speak of the Ribble, valley of my birth . . . I'm counting on you, Grandmaster of the spoken word . . . As for myself and my faithful companion, after long years of labour in the name of humanity wherein we fought for a just cause, it only remains for us to make an immediate exit, to make the supreme sacrifice at no one's instigation but our own . . .

Old Woman (*sobbing*) Yes – let's die gloriously . . . let's die and go down in legend . . . At the very least they'll give us a blue plaque . . .

Old Man Sémiramis! Faithful companion! . . . Who has unquestioningly believed in me for nearly a century. Who

54

has never once left me . . . Today – unfortunately – at the climactic moment, the pitiless crowd divides us . . .

If only we
could somehow be
laid beneath stones
as one bag of bones.
If worms could only share
our flesh, we'd swear
that death was overcome –
and rot as one . . .

Old Woman . . . and rot as one . . .

Old Man But unfortunately . . .

Old Woman Unfortunately . . .

Old Man . . . our bodies will fall far apart and rot in underwater isolation . . . But let's not complain.

Old Woman What must be done, must be done! . . .

Old Man We will not be forgotten. The eternal Emperor will remember us for ever.

Old Woman (*echo*) For ever.

Old Man We will leave our mark, since we are people, not cities.

Old Man and Old Woman (*together*) We will have a blue plaque!

Old Man If we cannot be united in space – as we were in adversity – then let us be united in time and for eternity. Let us die at the same instant . . . (*to the impassive, motionless Orator*) One last time . . . I believe in you . . . I'm counting on you . . . to say everything . . . to bequeath the message . . . (*to Emperor*) Your Majesty must excuse me . . . Farewell to you all. Farewell, Sémiramis.

Old Woman Farewell to you all! . . . Farewell my poppet!

Old Man Long live the Emperor!

The Old Man throws confetti and streamers over the invisible Emperor. We hear fanfares. Brilliant light – like fireworks.

Old Woman Long live the Emperor!

Confetti and streamers in the direction of the Emperor – then over the motionless impassive Orator – over the empty chairs.

Old Man (*doing the same*) Long live the King of Kings!

Old Woman (*doing the same*) Long live the King of Kings!

Simultaneously the Old Woman and the Old Man throw themselves out of their respective windows, shouting 'Long live the Emperor'. A sudden silence. No more fireworks. We hear an 'Ah' from both sides of the stage, then the sickly sound of bodies falling into the water. The light from the windows and the big door has vanished. All that remains is the faint light as at the opening. The windows, black holes, remain wide open. The curtains flap in the breeze.

The Orator, who has remained motionless and impassive during this scene of double-suicide, decides after a few moments to speak. Facing the rows of empty chairs, he gives the invisible crowd to understand that he is deaf and dumb. He makes signs in deaf and dumb language – desperate attempts to make himself understood. Then he produces the guttural groans and rasps of the mute.

Orator He, mme, mm, mm.
Ju, gou, hou, hou.

Heu, heu, gu, gou, gueue. (*Defeated, he lets his arms fall to his sides. Suddenly his face lights up: an idea. He turns to the blackboard, takes a chalk from his pocket and writes in big capital letters.*)

ANGELSWEEP

Then:

NNA NNM NWNWNW V

He turns back to the invisible audience on the stage and points to what he has written.

Mmm, mmm, gueue, gou, gu, mmm, mmm, mmm, mmmm. (*Then, dissatisfied, he violently rubs out the chalk marks, and replaces them with others, still in big capitals, among which can be made out:*)

XP ΛGOD IS ΛGONE IΣ

Once more the Orator turns back to the room. He smiles questioningly, apparently hoping to have been understood, to have said something. He points out what he has just written to the empty chairs. For a few moments he remains motionless, a little solemn, reasonably happy. Then, not getting the hoped-for reaction, his smile gradually fades and his face darkens. He waits a moment more, then abruptly he bad-temperedly takes his leave and gets off the rostrum. He goes towards the big door at the back with his ghostly walk. Before leaving he once more, and with ceremony, takes his leave of the empty rows of chairs, of the invisible Emperor. The stage remains empty – the chairs, the rostrum, the floor covered in streamers and confetti. The door at the back is wide open on to black.

For the first time we hear human noises from the invisible crowd: bursts of laughter, muttering, 'shush'ing, ironic coughing. Faint at first, these sounds will grow before gradually once more dying away. All this should last long enough for the audience – real and visible – to leave with this ending etched in their minds. Very slowly the curtain falls.[5]

April–June 1951

Ionesco's Notes

1 These yes's and no's should begin slowly and rhythmi-
cally, like a monotonous chant – then accelerate, their
heads doddering gently in time.

2 This line cut in performance – as well as the following
stage direction. There was no table.

3 The number of chairs brought on stage is clearly
important – a good forty at least – more if possible. They
come on thick and fast. They pile up. The stage should be
invaded by these chairs – this crowd of present absences.
For this reason (rhythm, speed) it's better if the Old
Woman is played by a young actress made up. This was
what was done in Paris (Tsilla Chelton) and in London
and New York (Joan Plowright) It should be a *tour de
force*, rather like a circus act. At the end of this section,
chairs may equally appear at the back of the set. By
means of lighting the old couple's small room should seem
to have grown immense, like a cathedral. This is how it
looked in the *mise en scène* by Jacques Mauclair (1956)
thanks to Jacques Noel's design.

    The Old Woman's lines, when she is repeating the Old
Man's last words, are sometimes like much louder echoes,
but sometimes should be spoken as a chant or rhythmic
lamentation.

    After a certain point the chairs no longer represent
fixed characters (Lady, Field Marshal, Fabled Beauty,
Offsetlithographer, etc.), but the whole crowd. They take
on their own life. [*Elles jouent toutes seules.*]

    This is why I emphasize that the director, while the final
wave of chairs is arriving, should allow the panic-stricken

Old Woman to bring them on without speaking, for one minute. During this minute, while the relentless ringing is the only sound, the Old Man down-stage, puppet-like, can simply make rapid bows – right, left, ahead – to welcome the guests.

We had even envisaged using a second Old Woman with a figure identical to Sémiramis, who could bring on chairs at the moment of acceleration, always keeping her back to us, immediately appearing on one side of the stage when Sémiramis had just gone out on the other – giving an impression of speed and of Sémiramis and the chairs being everywhere at once. This second Old Woman might do this once or twice. This could give a feeling of simultaneity, with the Old Woman appearing to enter from one side just as she has exited from the other, and vice versa.

4 The Old Man's speech from 'Listen Your Majesty . . . I had a revelation' to 'took the place of a mother and father' was cut in the original performance. I advise it remains cut.

5 In [the first] performance, the curtain fell with the groaning of the dumb Orator. The blackboard was cut.

There was no music when this play was first performed in 1952. For the second production by Mauclair (1956, revived 1961) Pierre Barbaud composed musical fragments for us – notably for the Emperor's entrance (fanfares), the frenetic arrival of chairs, and particularly for the ending, when the old couple are thanking everyone – derisory, triumphal, fairground music underscoring the irony, simultaneously tragic and grotesque, of what the two actors are playing.